FIRST EDITION

Edited By: **Kelly Hanton**

Designed By: **Anthony Brown** and **Natalie Lindsey**

Acknowledgments

Writing this book has been a journey, and I wouldn't have reached the finish line without the support of many incredible people.

First and foremost, my deepest gratitude goes to my **[partner Sophia Ava]**, who provided unwavering encouragement, endless cups of coffee, and sanity checks throughout the writing process. Their love and patience were invaluable.

My sincere thanks to my **editor, [Kelly Hanton]**, for your keen eye, insightful suggestions, and guidance in shaping this book. Your expertise made a world of difference.

I am also grateful to my agents, for believing in this project and helping me navigate the publishing world. Your support and professionalism were instrumental.

Many thanks to my **friends and colleagues** who offered feedback on early drafts, shared their knowledge, and celebrated the milestones with me. Your enthusiasm and support kept me motivated.

A special thank you to **[anyone who provided specific help, e.g., research assistance, illustrations, blurbs]**. Your contribution is greatly appreciated.

Finally, thank you to the **readers**. This book exists for you. I hope you find it informative, inspiring, or simply enjoyable.

CONTENT

Biking Trails

Campgrounds

How to use this book

The first section of the book is a layout map. This map depicts the natural features of the land, including mountains, valleys, trails, and bodies of water. By studying the map, you can plan your route, estimate the distance and elevation gain, and anticipate any challenging terrain.

By using a compass together with this guide, you can determine locations and navigate through unfamiliar terrain. This is especially important if you veer off course or encounter unexpected obstacles.

The section on hiking covers crucial aspects of a hiking trail

Including:

- **Trailhead location**
- **Description**
- **Difficulty**
- **Day Hike/Multi Day Hike**
- **Dog/Kid Friendly**
- **Type of hike**
- **Elevation change**
- **Length**
- **Estimated time to complete**
- **Features**
- **Allowed uses**
- **Best time to hike**
- **Tips**

It is important to note that some of these parameters may vary depending on several aspects:

Trail Length

A trail length depends on the starting point and end point used when measuring and may vary from one source to another. At times trail lengths can change over time due to erosion, rerouting, or construction.

The way the trail length is measured can vary. Some sources might use a GPS track, which could account for every twist and turn, while others might rely on a ranger's estimate or a historical map, which might be less precise.

Difficulty

The difficulty of a trail is typically determined by a combination of factors, including:

Terrain: How rough or smooth is the path? Is it mostly dirt, rock, roots, or pavement? Are there obstacles like streams, boulders, or steep drop-offs?

Elevation gain: How much climbing is involved? A steeper or longer climb will be more difficult.

Distance: How far is the total hike? A longer hike will naturally require more endurance.

Exposure: Are there sections of the trail where you'll be high up and at risk of a fall, with no railing or protection?

Trailhead location

Trailhead location might be moved due to many reasons some common factors are:

Safety: This is a big one. If the area around the old trailhead becomes unsafe due to things like erosion, flooding, or danger from falling rocks, park services might have to reroute the trail to a new starting point.

Conservation: Sometimes, a trailhead needs to be moved to protect the environment. If the old trailhead was disturbing wildlife habitat or a sensitive ecosystem, park rangers might create a new trailhead in a less disruptive location.

Estimated time to complete

There are many reasons why estimates for hiking trail completion times can vary so much, even for the same trail. Most common reasons are:

Hiker ability: This is a big one. An experienced hiker with good fitness will move much faster than someone new to hiking or who is out of shape.

Trail conditions: Mud, snow, rocks, and overgrown trails can all slow you down considerably. Weather can also play a big role - rain, wind, and extreme heat can all make a hike more difficult.

Pace: Are you stopping often to take breaks or pictures? Are you hiking with a group that needs to go slower than you might like? All of this can affect your overall time.

Elevation gain: This is a big one - the more elevation you gain, the longer it will take to complete the hike.

Taking breaks: Factoring in breaks for lunch, taking photos, or just enjoying the view is important. Don't forget to schedule some rest time into your hike.

Every effort has been made by the author and editors to make this guide as accurate as possible. However, many things can change after a guide is published i.e. trails may be rerouted or washed away by nature, roads may be closed and many other possibilities. **WE HOPE ALL THE USERS UNDERSTAND THIS!!**

Introduction

Welcome to a world of shifting sands, towering dunes, and serene shores. Indiana Dunes National Park is more than just a pretty face. It's a place where the heartland meets the Great Lakes, offering a unique blend of rugged beauty and unexpected adventure.

A Tapestry of Terrain

If you're a hiker, you're in for a treat. The park offers a diverse landscape that will keep your legs burning and your spirit soaring. From the gentle slopes of the beach to the challenging climbs of the dunes, there's a trail for every skill level.

- **The Dunes:** These aren't your average sandhills. Some rise as high as 190 feet, offering breathtaking views of Lake Michigan. Hiking through the dunes is like walking on another planet. The shifting sands create a constantly changing environment, making every hike a new experience.

- **The Marshes:** A hidden gem of the park, the marshes are home to a rich array of wildlife. Trails wind through this watery wonderland, offering glimpses of herons, turtles, and even the elusive otter. It's a peaceful escape from the hustle and bustle.

- **The Forests:** While the dunes and marshes steal the show, the park's forests are equally enchanting. Tall oak and hickory trees create a canopy of green, providing shade on hot summer days. Keep an eye out for deer, squirrels, and other forest dwellers.

A Hiker's Dream

Whether you're a seasoned trailblazer or a casual wanderer, Indiana Dunes has something to offer.

- **Short and Sweet:** For a quick escape, try the Dune Succession Trail. It's a short but informative hike that showcases the park's ecological diversity.

- **Challenge Accepted:** If you're up for a workout, the Glenwood Dunes Trail is a must-do. This steep climb will test your endurance, but the views from the top are worth every step.

- **Nature Lover's Delight:** The Cowles Bog Trail offers a glimpse into the park's wetland ecosystem. It's a peaceful hike where you can observe a variety of plant and animal life.

Beyond the Trails

Hiking isn't the only thing to do in Indiana Dunes. Take a dip in Lake Michigan, explore the historic Bailly Homestead, or simply relax on the beach and watch the sunset. The park offers endless opportunities for recreation and relaxation.

So, what are you waiting for? Grab your hiking boots, pack your water bottle, and get ready to discover the magic of Indiana Dunes National Park. It's a place where you can escape the ordinary and connect with nature.

Geology, History & Wildlife

Geology:

Indiana Dunes National Park is a testament to the raw power of nature, shaped over millennia by the relentless forces of ice and water. The park's dramatic landscape is a result of the interplay between glaciers and the Great Lakes.

- **Glacial Legacy:** During the last ice age, massive glaciers advanced and retreated, sculpting the land and depositing vast quantities of sediment. The park's rolling hills, valleys, and moraines are remnants of this glacial period.

- **Lake Michigan's Influence:** As the glaciers receded, Lake Michigan formed, its waves and winds shaping the shoreline and creating the iconic sand dunes. Over time, these dunes have migrated inland, creating unique ecosystems and breathtaking vistas.

- **Dynamic Dunes:** The park's dunes are constantly changing, shaped by wind and water. Blowouts, where wind erodes the dunes, reveal layers of history, including buried forests and ancient shorelines.

History:

The Indiana Dunes region has a rich and complex history, shaped by both natural forces and human activity.

- **Indigenous Peoples:** The area was originally inhabited by Native American tribes, who relied on the lake and surrounding land for sustenance. Evidence of their presence can still be found throughout the park.

- **Industrial Development:** The late 19th and early 20th centuries saw rapid industrialization along the shores of Lake Michigan, including the establishment of steel mills and other heavy industries. This period of development posed significant environmental challenges to the dunes.

- **Conservation Efforts:** Recognizing the ecological importance of the dunes, conservationists and activists fought to protect the area from further development. Their efforts culminated in the establishment of Indiana Dunes National Park in 2019, preserving this unique ecosystem for future generations.

Wildlife:

Indiana Dunes National Park is a haven for a diverse array of plant and animal life. Its unique blend of habitats, from sandy shores to wetlands and forests, supports a rich tapestry of biodiversity.

- **Flora:** The park boasts a variety of plant communities, including beach grasses, oak-hickory forests, and wetlands. Rare and endangered species, such as the Pitcher's thistle, find refuge here.

- **Fauna:** The park is home to a diverse range of wildlife, including birds, mammals, reptiles, amphibians, and insects. Visitors may encounter deer, coyotes, foxes, and a variety of bird species, including bald eagles. The park's wetlands support amphibians and reptiles, while the shoreline provides habitat for fish and aquatic birds.

How to Prepare

Before You Go

- **Research:** Familiarize yourself with the park's layout, trails, and activities that interest you. The park's official website is a great resource.

- **Check Weather:** Indiana weather can be unpredictable. Check the forecast before your trip and pack accordingly.

- **Obtain Permits:** While most activities don't require permits, some, like camping or group events, might. Check the park's website for specific requirements.

- **Plan Your Itinerary:** Decide how many days you'll spend, what activities you want to do, and where you'll stay. Consider creating a flexible itinerary to accommodate unexpected weather or discoveries.

- **Book Accommodations:** If you're planning to stay overnight, book your accommodations in advance, especially during peak season. Options include campgrounds, hotels, and vacation rentals.

When to Visit

- **Peak Season (Summer):** This is the busiest time, with warm weather perfect for swimming and sunbathing. Expect larger crowds and higher prices.
- **Shoulder Seasons (Spring and Fall):** Offers pleasant weather, fewer crowds, and stunning foliage in autumn.

- **Winter:** While the park is less crowded, some amenities may be closed. However, it's a great time for winter hiking and exploring the frozen dunes.

Getting There

- **By Car:** The park is easily accessible by car. Major highways lead to the area.
- **By Air:** The nearest major airports are Chicago O'Hare International Airport (ORD) and Chicago Midway International Airport (MDW). From there, you can rent a car or take public transportation.

What to Pack

- **Essential Gear:** Hiking shoes, comfortable clothing, sunscreen, hat, sunglasses, insect repellent, water bottle, and a camera.

- **Beach Essentials:** Swimsuit, towel, beach chair, and any beach toys.

- **Optional Gear:** Binoculars for birdwatching, a guidebook for identifying plants and wildlife, and a first-aid kit.

- **Clothing:** Layer your clothing as the weather can be unpredictable. Pack for both warm and cool temperatures.

Things to Do

- **Hiking:** Explore the diverse trails, ranging from easy to challenging. Don't miss the iconic Mount Baldy.

- **Beach Activities:** Relax on the sandy shores of Lake Michigan, swim, sunbathe, or build sandcastles.

- **Wildlife Watching:** Keep an eye out for various bird species, deer, and other wildlife.

- **Outdoor Recreation:** Enjoy kayaking, paddleboarding, biking, and fishing.

- **Visitor Centers:** Learn about the park's history and ecology at the Paul H. Douglas Center for Environmental Education.

- **Photography:** Capture the stunning beauty of the dunes, beaches, and wildlife.

Additional Tips:

- Respect the environment: Stay on designated trails, pack out your trash, and leave no trace.

- Be aware of your surroundings: Watch for changing weather conditions and potential hazards like steep dunes.

- Bring enough water: Stay hydrated, especially on hot days.

- Enjoy the experience: Relax and soak in the natural beauty of Indiana Dunes National Park.

Rules and Regulations

1. Do not injure or damage any structure, rock, tree, flower, bird or wild animal. Do NOT gather limbs, brush or trees (either dead or alive) for firewood because they rebuild the natural humus.

2. Any firearm (except lawfully possessed handguns), BB gun, air gun, CO2 gun, bow and arrow, paint gun or spear gun in possession in a state park must be unloaded or un-nocked and stored in a case or locked within a vehicle, except when owner is participating in an activity authorized by written permit.

3. Dogs and cats must be attended at all times and kept on a leash no longer than 6 feet.

4. Vending or advertising without permission of the Department of Natural Resources is prohibited.

5. Camping is permitted only in the campground. Youth groups must be under adult supervision. No youth groups permitted in the family campground. Campers must be 18 to register for a campsite.

6. Fires shall be built only in designated places.

7. Please comply with the Carry In/Carry Out trash policy in all day-use areas. Overnight guests must put waste in receptacles provided for that purpose.

8. Motorists shall observe posted speed limits and park only in designated areas.

9. Swimming is limited to places and times designated by the Department of Natural Resources.

10. Drinking water should be taken only from pumps, hydrants or fountains provided for that purpose.

11. Report lost or found articles to the park office.

12. All-terrain vehicles are prohibited in the park.

13. Metal detectors are allowed on the beach from September to May, with written permission from the property manager.

LAKE MICHIGAN

GARY

HOBART

PORTAGE

CHESTERTON

MICHIGAN CITY

Paul H. Douglas Center
for Environmental Education

West Beach

Portage Lakefront
and Riverwalk

Indiana Dunes
State Park

INDIANA DUNES
STATE PARK

Indiana Dunes Visitor Center

Porter Access Point

Kemil Road Access Point

Dunbar Access Point

Central Avenue Access Point

Mount Baldy

Lake View

Dunewood
Campground

Heron Rookery

Pinhook Bog

North

Indiana Dunes National Lakeshore boundary extends
1/4 mile into Lake Michigan and National Park Service
regulations apply.

Hiking Trails

Bailly Homestead / Chellberg Farm Trail

Trailhead

Bailly / Chellberg parking lot within the park.

Description

This trail offers a blend of history, nature, and easy walking. You'll explore a historic homestead, a working farm, and diverse ecosystems.

Difficulty

Easy to moderate. There are some changes in elevation and stairs, but overall, it's accessible for most hikers.

Type of Hike

Loop or out and back, depending on the route you choose. There are several interconnected trails.

Elevation Change

Minimal elevation change, making it suitable for most fitness levels.

Dogs are allowed on leash.

The trail is perfect for families with children of all ages.

Length

- Outer Loop: 3.4 miles

- Bailly/Chellberg Inner Loop: 1.1 miles

Estimated Time to Complete

45 minutes to 2.5 hours, depending on the chosen route and pace.

Accessibility

The trail is generally accessible, with some sections featuring stairs and boardwalks. There are covered picnic shelters near the parking lot that are wheelchair accessible.

Equipment Needed

Comfortable hiking shoes, water, sunscreen, insect repellent, and possibly binoculars for birdwatching.

Ability

Suitable for most people, including families and those new to hiking.

Features

- Historic Bailly Homestead
- Working Chellberg Farm
- Diverse ecosystems (forest, prairie, river)
- Scenic views
- Educational opportunities

Allowed Uses

Hiking, walking, nature observation, photography. Bicycles and motorized vehicles are prohibited.

Trail Surface

Packed soil with wood chips in places, and several sets of stairs. Can be wet and muddy.

Best Time to Hike

Spring and fall offer pleasant temperatures and vibrant colors. Summer can be hot and humid, while winter can be cold and icy.

Tips

Choose your loop: Decide if you want to hike the entire 3.4-mile outer loop or the shorter 1.1-mile inner loop.

Check weather conditions: The trail can be muddy after rain, so wear appropriate footwear.

Bring water and snacks: There's no water on the trail, so stay hydrated.

Wildlife encounters: Keep an eye out for birds, squirrels, and other wildlife.

Photography: Capture the beauty of the forest, river, and historic buildings.

Parking: There is a parking lot at the trailhead with restrooms and picnic areas.

Accessibility: The trail is generally accessible, but there are some stairs and uneven terrain.

Exploring the Area:

- **Bailly Homestead:** Learn about the early French settlers and explore the historic buildings.

- **Chellberg Farm:** Discover the history of Swedish immigrants and the farm's role in the community.

- **Little Calumet River:** Enjoy the scenic views of the river and its surrounding wetlands.

- **Mnoké Prairie:** Experience a glimpse of the region's original grasslands.

Bailly Homestead

The Chellberg farmhouse

Little Calumet River and Mnoké Prairie Trails

Trailhead

The trailhead is located at the Bailly Homestead and Chellberg Farm area.

Description

This trail system offers a diverse experience, taking hikers through hardwood forests, along the Little Calumet River, and across the restored Mnoké Prairie. It provides a glimpse into the area's rich history and natural beauty.

Difficulty

Moderate. WhIle there are some flat sections, the trail also includes gentle inclines and declines.

Type of Hike

Loop. The trail forms a loop, allowing hikers to return to the starting point.

Elevation Change

Moderate elevation changes throughout the trail.

Dogs are allowed on leash.

The trail is generally kid-friendly, but younger children might need assistance in some areas.

Length

Approximately 3.9 miles.

Estimated Time to Complete

1-2 hours, depending on pace and stops.

Accessibility

The trail is generally accessible, but some sections may be challenging for individuals with mobility impairments.

Equipment Needed

Sturdy hiking shoes, water, sunscreen, insect repellent, and a map or guide.

Ability

Moderate fitness level is recommended.

Features

- Scenic views of the Little Calumet River and Mnoké Prairie

- Diverse ecosystems

- Historical sites (Bailly Homestead and Chellberg Farm)

- Opportunity for wildlife viewing

Allowed Uses

Hiking, birding, nature observation.

Trail Surface

A mix of dirt, gravel, and boardwalk.

Best Time to Hike

Spring and fall offer pleasant temperatures and vibrant colors. Summer can be hot and humid, while winter may be cold and icy in some areas.

Tips

- **Trail Conditions:** The trail can be muddy after rain, so wear appropriate footwear.
- **Diverse Ecosystem:** Experience a variety of habitats, including woodlands, prairies, and riverbanks.
- **Wildlife:** Keep an eye out for birds, deer, and other wildlife.
- **Historical Sites:** Explore the Bailly Homestead and Chellberg Farm for a glimpse into the area's past.
- **Photography Opportunities:** Capture stunning shots of the river, prairie, and surrounding landscapes.
- **Birding:** The area is known for its bird diversity, so bring binoculars if you're interested in birdwatching.

- **Picnicking:** Enjoy a leisurely picnic at one of the designated areas.

Iron Horse Heritage Trail

Trailhead

There are two primary trailheads:

- **Imagination Glen Park:** Located at 2275 McCool Road.

- **Steel Wheels BMX Track:** Located on State Road 149, 0.75 miles south of US 20.

Description

The Iron Horse Heritage Trail is a paved, linear trail that follows the path of a former railroad. It offers a scenic route through a greenway corridor, with wooded areas and glimpses of suburban life.

Difficulty

Easy. The trail is primarily flat and paved, making it suitable for most fitness levels.

Type of Hike

Out and back. The trail extends in both directions from the trailheads.

Elevation Change

Minimal elevation change. The trail is relatively flat.

Dogs are allowed on leash.

The trail is wide, flat, and easy to navigate, making it perfect for families.

Length

Approximately 4.8 miles round trip.

Estimated Time to Complete

1-2 hours, depending on pace.

Accessibility

The paved surface makes the trail accessible to most people, including those with mobility challenges.

Equipment Needed

Comfortable walking shoes or bike (for cycling), water, sunscreen, and insect repellent.

Ability

Suitable for all ages and fitness levels.

Features

- Scenic views of the greenway corridor
- Connection to Imagination Glen Park and Woodland Park
- Potential for wildlife sightings

Allowed Uses

Hiking, biking, running, and walking.

Trail Surface

Paved.

Best Time to Hike

Spring, summer, and fall offer pleasant hiking conditions. Avoid winter if icy conditions are present.

Note: While the Iron Horse Heritage Trail is not technically within Indiana Dunes National Park, it is a popular starting point for exploring the park's trails.

Tips

- **Parking:** You can park at Imagination Glen Park or the Steel Wheels BMX Track.
- **Trail Conditions:** The trail is primarily paved and easy to navigate, making it suitable for all ages and fitness levels.
- **Wildlife:** Keep an eye out for various bird species and other small wildlife that call the area home.
- **Connect with Nature:** Take a moment to appreciate the surrounding greenery, especially the wooded areas.
- **Combine with Other Trails:** Consider extending your adventure by connecting to the Prairie Duneland Trail for a longer ride or walk.
- **Bicycles Welcome:** The trail is popular among cyclists, so be aware of other users.
- **Amenities:** There are no restrooms or water fountains along the trail.

Calumet Dunes Trail

Trailhead

Parking lot trailhead, intersection of Kemil Road and US Highway 12, Chesterton, IN.

Description

The Calumet Dunes Trail is a short, paved loop that provides a glimpse into the history of the area. It follows the Calumet Dunes ridge, an ancient shoreline of Lake Michigan.

Difficulty

Easy with some elevation change.

Type of Hike

Loop

Elevation Change

Moderate elevation change.

Dogs are welcomed but must be on a leash (6 feet or shorter).

The trail is very kid-friendly.

Length

0.5 miles

Estimated Time to Complete

20 minutes

Accessibility

Wheelchair accessible.

Equipment Needed

Comfortable walking shoes, water, sunscreen, insect repellent.

Ability

Suitable for all ages and fitness levels.

Features

Scenic views of the dunes, potential wildlife sightings.

Allowed Uses

Hiking, walking, running, wheelchair accessible.

Trail Surface

Paved.

Best Time to Hike

Spring, summer, and fall offer pleasant hiking conditions. Winter can be enjoyable for cross-country skiing.

Note: While this trail is a great introduction to the park, it's just a small part of what Indiana Dunes National Park offers. Consider exploring other trails for a more in-depth experience.

Tips

- **Start counterclockwise:** This will help you stay on the right path.
- **Be aware of trail junctions:** There are a few junctions, so pay attention to the signs.
- **Enjoy the views:** Take breaks to admire the dune formations and surrounding landscape.
- **Wildlife watching:** Keep an eye out for birds, squirrels, and other wildlife.
- **Pack accordingly:** Bring water, sunscreen, and insect repellent, especially during warmer months.
- **Respect the environment:** Stay on the trail to protect the delicate ecosystem.
- There are restrooms and potable water available year-round.

Calumet Dunes Trail

Cowles Bog Trail

Trailhead

There are two trailheads:

- **North Trailhead:** Main parking lot, gravel surface.

- **South Trailhead:** Greenbelt, paved parking lot.

Description

The Cowles Bog Trail is a remarkable 4.7-mile trail that winds through diverse ecosystems, including marshes, swamps, black oak savannas, and eventually reaches the shores of Lake Michigan. It's named after Dr. Henry Cowles, a pioneer in plant ecology who conducted significant research in this area.

Difficulty

Moderate to Rugged. The trail involves climbing steep sand dunes, which can be challenging.

Type of Hike

Out and back

Elevation Change

Approximately 202 feet

Dogs are welcomed but must be on a leash (6 feet or shorter).

Older kids who are physically fit can enjoy the trail, but it might be challenging for younger children due to the steep dunes and varying terrain.

Length

4.7 miles

Estimated Time to Complete

Approximately 4 hours

Accessibility

The trail is not accessible for people with disabilities due to the steep terrain and loose sand.

Equipment Needed

Sturdy hiking shoes, water, sunscreen, insect repellent, and possibly hiking poles for dune climbing.

Ability

Moderate fitness level is recommended due to the steep dunes and varying terrain.

Features

- Scenic views of Lake Michigan
- Diverse ecosystems (marshes, swamps, black oak savannas)
- Opportunity to learn about plant ecology

Allowed Uses

Hiking

Trail Surface

Mixture of loose sand and packed dirt

Best Time to Hike

Spring and fall offer pleasant temperatures and vibrant foliage. Summer can be hot and humid, while winter can be cold and snowy.

Tips

Consider bug repellent: Depending on the time of year, mosquitoes and other insects can be present.

Check for park closures or restrictions: Be aware of any temporary closures or regulations.

Stay on the trail: Protect delicate ecosystems by staying on designated paths.

Be mindful of wildlife: Observe wildlife from a distance and avoid disturbing their habitat.

Pack out what you pack in: Help preserve the park's beauty by leaving no trace.

Take your time: Enjoy the scenery and wildlife.

Bring binoculars: If you're interested in birdwatching, binoculars can enhance your experience

Explore the bog: Cowles Bog is a unique ecosystem. Take time to observe the plants and wildlife that call it home.

Enjoy the beach: The trail leads to a secluded beach. Pack a picnic and relax.

Consider combining with other trails: For a longer hike, consider connecting with other trails in the park.

Views of Lake Michigan from Cowles Bog

Dune Ridge Trail

Location

North of U.S. Highway 12 on East State Park Road (300E), Beverly Shores, IN 46301.

Trailhead

The trailhead is located in the large beach parking lot off State Park Road.

Description

The Dune Ridge Trail offers a diverse ecosystem experience in a relatively short distance. You'll traverse through foredunes, oak savanna, and enjoy views of wetlands and forests.

Difficulty

Moderate. The trail involves some steep slopes on loose sand, which can be challenging.

Type of Hike

Out and back with a loop option.

Elevation Change

73 feet.

Dogs are welcomed but, on a leash, (6 feet or shorter).

Kids are welcomed but with adult supervision due to the loose sand and some steep sections.

Length

0.7 miles.

Estimated Time to Complete

30 minutes to 1 hour.

Accessibility

The trail is not accessible for everyone due to the terrain.

Equipment Needed

Sturdy hiking shoes, water, sunscreen, and insect repellent.

Ability

Moderate fitness level is recommended.

Features

Scenic views, diverse ecosystems, and opportunities for wildlife observation.

Allowed Uses

Hiking only. Bicycles and motorized vehicles are prohibited.

Trail Surface

Mixture of loose sand and packed dirt.

Best Time to Hike

Spring and fall offer pleasant temperatures and fewer crowds. However, the trail is enjoyable year-round.

Wear appropriate footwear: Hiking boots or sturdy sneakers with good ankle support are recommended due to the varying terrain.

Bring water and snacks: Even though the hike is short, staying hydrated is important, especially during warmer months.

Respect wildlife: Keep a safe distance from animals and avoid disturbing their habitat.

What to Expect:

- **Diverse ecosystem:** Experience the transition from sandy dunes to oak savannas and wetlands.

- **Stunning views:** Enjoy panoramic views of the surrounding area from the top of the dune.

- **Wildlife encounters:** Keep an eye out for various bird species, deer, and other wildlife.

- **Moderate difficulty:** The trail involves some steep slopes and loose sand, so be prepared for a workout.

Glenwood Dunes Trails

Location

The Glenwood Dunes Trail system is located within Indiana Dunes National Park, near Chesterton, Indiana.

Trailhead

There are two primary trailheads:

- **Glenwood Dunes Trailhead:** Located at the intersection of US Highway 20 and Brummitt Road.
- **Calumet Dunes Trailhead:** Also accessible from the park.

Description

The Glenwood Dunes Trails offer an extensive network of interconnected loops ranging from less than a mile to nearly 15 miles. The trails wind through diverse landscapes, including towering sand dunes, wetlands, forests, and open prairies.

Difficulty

Easy to moderate: While there are some elevation changes, the trails are generally considered accessible to hikers of various fitness levels.

Type of Hike

Loop: The trail system is primarily made up of interconnected loops, allowing hikers to customize their routes based on time and preference.

Elevation Change

Moderate: Expect some elevation gain as you climb the dunes.

Dogs are allowed on most of the trails, but they must be leashed. However, they are prohibited on the equestrian portion of the trail for safety reasons.

The trails are suitable for kids of all ages, but supervision is recommended, especially when exploring the dunes.

Length

Less than 1 mile to 6.8 miles: The extensive trail system offers options for various hiking distances.

Estimated Time to Complete

Less than 1 hour to 4 hours: The hiking time depends on the chosen route and pace.

Accessibility

The trails are generally accessible, with some sections featuring boardwalks. However, climbing sand dunes can be challenging for individuals with mobility limitations.

Equipment Needed

- Sturdy hiking shoes
- Water
- Sunscreen
- Insect repellent
- Map or GPS
- Camera (optional)

Ability

Beginner to intermediate: Hikers of all levels can enjoy the Glenwood Dunes Trails.

Features

- **Scenic:** The trails offer stunning views of Lake Michigan, sand dunes, and diverse ecosystems.

- **Kids and families:** The park is a great place for family outings and outdoor recreation.

Allowed Uses

- Hiking, running, horseback riding (on designated trails), cross-country skiing (in winter)

Trail Surface

- **Packed dirt, sand, and boardwalk:** The trail conditions vary depending on the specific section.

Best Time to Hike

Spring and fall: These seasons offer pleasant temperatures and comfortable hiking conditions. Summer can be hot and humid, while winter may bring cold and snowy weather.

Tips

- **Choose your distance:** The trail system offers various loop options from less than a mile to nearly 15 miles. Determine your desired hike length based on your fitness level and available time.
- **Explore different seasons:** Each season offers unique beauty. Fall foliage, winter snow, spring blooms, and summer sun all create different atmospheres.
- **Consider horseback riding:** The trails are open to horseback riding during certain months.

- **Combine with other activities:** After your hike, enjoy a picnic, beach time, or visit the nearby towns for shopping and dining.
- **Be aware of your surroundings:** Stay on marked trails and be cautious of changing weather conditions.
- **Inform someone of your plans:** Let a friend or family member know where you're going and when you expect to return.
- **Carry a phone:** A charged phone can be a lifesaver in case of emergencies.

Great Marsh Trail

Location

The Great Marsh Trail is located in Beverly Shores, Indiana, within the Indiana Dunes National Park.

Trailhead

The main trailhead is at the south parking lot. There is also a north parking lot, but the main trailhead is at the south.

Description

The Great Marsh Trail offers a serene escape into a restored wetland ecosystem. It's a popular trail for birdwatching, as it's home to a diverse array of avian species. The trail leads to an observation deck providing stunning views of the marsh.

Difficulty

Easy. There is no significant elevation change, making it suitable for hikers of all ages and fitness levels.

Type of Hike

Out and back or **loop**. The trail can be hiked as an out-and-back to the observation deck or as a loop by following the trail markers.

Elevation Change

Minimal. The trail is relatively flat.

Dogs are allowed on leashes (6 feet or shorter).

The easy terrain and opportunity to spot wildlife make it a great trail for families.

Length

Approximately 1.3 miles.

Estimated Time to Complete

Around 1 hour.

Accessibility

The trail is generally accessible, with a paved path leading to the observation deck. However, some parts of the trail may be muddy or uneven.

Equipment Needed

- Sturdy hiking shoes

- Water

- Insect repellent

- Binoculars (optional for birdwatching)

Ability

Suitable for all levels of hikers.

Features

- Scenic marsh views

- Diverse birdlife

- Observation deck

- Kid and family-friendly

Allowed Uses

Hiking, birdwatching, photography. Bicycles and motorized vehicles are prohibited.

Trail Surface

Packed dirt and grass with some sections of gravel. The trail can be wet and muddy at times.

Best Time to Hike

The Great Marsh is beautiful year-round, but spring and fall offer the best opportunities for birdwatching. Avoid hiking during heavy rain or storms.

Tips

- **Spring Migration (April-May):** This is peak birding season when you'll see a wide variety of migratory birds.
- **Fall Migration (September-October):** Another excellent time to spot migrating birds, including sandhill cranes.
- **Be patient:** Birdwatching requires patience. Take your time and enjoy the peaceful surroundings.
- **Dress appropriately:** Layers are recommended as the weather can be unpredictable.
- **Respect wildlife:** Observe wildlife from a distance and avoid disturbing their habitat.

- **Use the observation deck:** The deck provides a great vantage point for viewing the marsh.
- **Combine with other trails:** For a longer adventure, consider combining the Great Marsh Trail with other nearby trails.
- There are no restrooms or potable water on the trail.
- The marsh is a delicate ecosystem, so please stay on the designated trails.

Great Marsh

Heron Rookery Trail

Location

The Heron Rookery Trail is located within Indiana Dunes National Park, a bit removed from the main park attractions along Lake Michigan. It's closer to the town of Michigan City, Indiana.

Trailhead

The trailhead is accessible from two parking lots:

- **Main (east) parking lot:** Large, gravel lot capable of accommodating buses and RVs.
- **Alternate (west) parking lot:** Smaller gravel lot with limited parking.

Description

The Heron Rookery Trail follows the Little Calumet River through a wooded area. While it was once a nesting ground for Great Blue Herons, the birds have since relocated. However, the trail still offers a serene woodland experience and is renowned for its stunning display of wildflowers in the spring.

Difficulty

Easy. The trail is flat with no significant elevation changes.

Type of Hike

Out and back.

Elevation Change

Minimal. The trail is relatively flat.

Dogs are welcomed but dogs must be leashed (6 feet or shorter).

The trail is easy and suitable for children.

Length

Approximately 3.3 miles.

Estimated Time to Complete

1.5 to 2 hours.

Accessibility

The trail surface is packed dirt and clay, which can be slippery and muddy, especially after rain. It might be challenging for those with mobility issues.

Equipment Needed

- Sturdy hiking shoes
- Water
- Insect repellent
- Camera (optional)

Ability

The trail is suitable for most people with average fitness levels.

Features

- Scenic woodland views
- Diverse birdlife
- Abundant wildflowers in spring

Allowed Uses

Hiking is the primary allowed use. Bicycles and motorized vehicles are prohibited.

Trail Surface

Packed dirt and clay.

Best Time to Hike

Spring is the most popular time to visit due to the stunning wildflowers. However, the trail is enjoyable throughout the year, offering different scenic beauty in each season.

Tips

What to Expect:

- **Diverse Birdlife:** Even though the herons have moved on, the area is still a haven for various bird species. Bring binoculars for a closer look.

- **Stunning Wildflowers:** Springtime offers an unforgettable display of wildflowers.

- **Peaceful Atmosphere:** Escape the crowds and enjoy the tranquility of the Little Calumet River.

- **Potential Mud:** The trail can be muddy, especially after rain. Wear appropriate footwear.

Wear comfortable hiking shoes: The trail can be uneven and muddy.
Bring water and snacks: There are no facilities on the trail.
Respect wildlife: Observe quietly and from a distance.
Check for ticks: This is a wooded area, so tick prevention is essential.
Consider a guided tour: If you want to learn more about the area, consider joining a guided hike.

Hobart Prairie Grove Trails

Location

Hobart Prairie Grove is located within the Indiana Dunes National Park, near the town of Hobart, Indiana.

Trailhead

The trailhead is located at Robinson Lake Park on South Liverpool Road.

Description

Hobart Prairie Grove offers a mix of forested ravines and open prairie landscapes. It's a great spot for birdwatching and enjoying nature's tranquility.

Difficulty

Easy. The trails are generally flat with minimal elevation change.

Type of Hike

- **Hobart Woodland Trail:** Out and back
- **Oak Savannah Rail Trail:** Out and back or loop

Elevation Change

Minimal elevation change.

Dogs are allowed on a leash (6 feet or shorter).

The trails are easy and suitable for kids.

Length

- **Hobart Woodland Trail:** 2.2 miles
- **Oak Savannah Rail Trail:** 2 miles within the park (part of a longer trail)

Estimated Time to Complete

Approximately 1.5 hours for the Hobart Woodland Trail. Time for the Oak Savannah Rail Trail will vary depending on distance covered.

Accessibility

The Oak Savannah Rail Trail is accessible for people with disabilities. The Hobart Woodland Trail may have some uneven terrain.

Equipment Needed

Sturdy hiking shoes, water, sunscreen, insect repellent.

Ability

Suitable for most fitness levels.

Features

- Scenic views of forested ravines and Lake George

- Diverse wildlife

- Opportunity for birdwatching

Allowed Uses

- Hiking

- Biking (Oak Savannah Rail Trail only)

Trail Surface

Packed dirt and clay. Can be wet and muddy at times.

Best Time to Hike

Spring and fall offer pleasant temperatures and vibrant colors. Summer can be hot and humid. Avoid winter for potential icy conditions.

Tips

Wear Appropriate Footwear: The trails can be muddy, so sturdy hiking boots or shoes with good traction are recommended.

Protect Yourself: Apply insect repellent to ward off ticks, especially during warmer months. Long pants and sleeves can also help.

Stay Hydrated: Bring plenty of water, especially on warmer days.

Respect Wildlife: Observe wildlife from a distance and avoid disturbing their habitat.

Hobart Woodland Trail:

- This trail offers a glimpse into a unique ecosystem.

- Watch for wildlife, especially birds.

- Be mindful of the terrain, as it can be uneven in some areas.

Oak Savannah Trail:

- This trail is shared with cyclists, so be aware of your surroundings.

- Enjoy the open prairie views and the chance to spot various bird species.

Hoosier Prairie Trail

Location

Hoosier Prairie is located in Schererville, Indiana, within the Indiana Dunes National Park.

Trailhead

The trailhead is located at the Hoosier Prairie parking lot, east of US Highway 41 on Main Street (53rd Avenue).

Description

Hoosier Prairie is a remnant of the once-common prairie landscape of northwest Indiana. This trail offers a unique opportunity to experience diverse ecosystems, including tallgrass prairie, marsh, and savanna. It's a great spot for observing wildlife and appreciating the beauty of native plants.

Difficulty

Easy

Type of Hike

- **Loop:** The trail system offers a loop trail that takes you through different habitats.
- **Out and back:** You can also choose to do an out and back hike on any of the segments.

Elevation Change

Minimal elevation change.

Dogs are allowed on leash.

The trail is easy and suitable for children.

Length

Approximately 0.7 miles for the entire loop.

Estimated Time to Complete

30 minutes to 1 hour.

Accessibility

The trail has a wheelchair-accessible portion, making it inclusive for all visitors.

Equipment Needed

- Sturdy walking shoes
- Water
- Insect repellent
- Sunscreen
- Camera (optional)

Ability

Suitable for all ages and fitness levels.

Features

- Scenic prairie landscape
- Diverse wildlife
- Wheelchair accessible

Allowed Uses

- Hiking
- Nature observation
- Photography

- Dog walking (on leash)

Trail Surface

Mixture of loose sand, packed dirt, and gravel.

Best Time to Hike

Spring and summer for wildflowers and wildlife viewing. Fall offers beautiful colors. Avoid hiking during hot, humid weather.

Tips

What to Expect:

- **Diverse Ecosystem:** Experience a variety of habitats, from dry oak savannas to wet prairies and marshes.

- **Abundant Wildlife:** Keep an eye out for birds, butterflies, and other prairie creatures.

- **Stunning Wildflowers:** Enjoy a colorful display of native plants, especially in spring and summer.

- **Tranquility:** Escape the crowds and immerse yourself in nature.

Trail Highlights:

- **Prairie Marsh Loop:** Immerse yourself in a pristine prairie and marsh environment.
- **Savanna Loop:** Explore a unique ecosystem with a mix of trees and prairie grasses.
- **Wheelchair Accessible Trail:** Enjoy the prairie's beauty without leaving your wheelchair.

Mount Baldy Beach Trail

Location

Indiana Dunes National Park, Porter County, Indiana, USA.

Trailhead

The trailhead is located at the Mount Baldy parking lot within Indiana Dunes National Park.

Description

The Mount Baldy Beach Trail offers a unique opportunity to experience the dynamic nature of the Indiana Dunes. The trail leads to the base of Mount Baldy, the largest moving dune in the park. While the summit is closed to the public, the beach below is accessible and offers stunning views of Lake Michigan.

Difficulty

Moderate to Rugged. The trail to the beach involves a steep descent through loose sand, making it challenging for some. The climb back up is equally strenuous.

Type of Hike

Out and back.

Elevation Change

Significant elevation change due to the steep descent to the beach.

Dogs are allowed on leash.

Older children who are physically fit can enjoy the hike. However, the steep terrain may be challenging for younger kids.

Length

0.75 miles.

Estimated Time to Complete

Approximately 1 hour.

Accessibility

The trail is not accessible for individuals with mobility impairments due to the steep terrain and loose sand.

Equipment Needed

Sturdy hiking shoes, water, sunscreen, and sunglasses.

Ability

Moderate fitness level required due to the steep terrain.

Features

- Scenic views of Lake Michigan
- Unique opportunity to experience a moving dune
- Beach access

Allowed Uses

Hiking.

Trail Surface

Packed dirt with sections of loose sand.

Best Time to Hike

Spring and fall offer pleasant hiking weather. Summer can be hot and crowded, while winter conditions can be challenging.

Tips

- The summit of Mount Baldy is closed to the public except during ranger-led programs.
- The dune and shoreline are constantly changing, so always obey trail markers and warning signs.
- Be cautious when hiking the beach, especially during high waves.
- Never walk out onto the shelf ice in winter.
- **Stay on the trail:** To protect the dune ecosystem, it's crucial to stay on designated trails.
- **Be cautious of steep slopes:** The descent to the beach is quite steep and the sand can be loose. Take your time and use caution.
- **Bring essentials:** Pack water, sunscreen, and a hat. You'll be exposed to the sun.
- **Respect wildlife:** Observe wildlife from a distance and avoid disturbing their habitat.
- **Mind the sand:** Sand can be difficult to climb, especially on the way back up. Take breaks if needed.
- **Consider timing:** Early morning or late afternoon can be less crowded and cooler.

Mount Baldy Sunrise

Views from Mount Baldy

Paul H. Douglas Trail (Miller Woods)

Location

Indiana Dunes National Park, Miller Woods, Gary, Indiana.

Trailhead

The trailhead is located at the Paul H. Douglas Center in Miller Woods.

Description

The Paul H. Douglas Trail, often referred to as the Miller Woods Trail, offers a diverse hiking experience through various ecosystems. You'll traverse wetlands, globally rare black oak savanna, open dunes, and eventually reach the shores of Lake Michigan. The trail is known for its stunning views of the lake and dunes, as well as its vibrant wildflowers, especially in spring.

Difficulty

Moderately challenging. The trail involves walking on sand, which can be tiring, and some sections have steeper inclines as you ascend the dunes.

Type of Hike

Out and back.

Elevation Change

Significant elevation change, especially as you climb the dunes.

Dogs are allowed on leash.

Suitable for older kids who are capable of hiking on sand and handling some elevation changes. Younger children might find the hike challenging.

Length

Approximately 3.5 miles.

Estimated Time to Complete

1-2 hours, depending on your pace and stops.

Accessibility

The trail is not accessible for wheelchairs or strollers due to sand and uneven terrain.

Equipment Needed

Sturdy hiking shoes, water, sunscreen, insect repellent, and a hat are recommended.

Ability

Moderate fitness level is required.

Features

- Scenic views of Lake Michigan and dunes
- Diverse ecosystems
- Wildflowers (especially in spring)
- Beach access

Allowed Uses

Hiking.

Trail Surface

Mostly sand, with some sections of packed soil, gravel, and boardwalk.

Best Time to Hike

Spring for wildflowers, summer for warm weather and beach activities, and fall for pleasant temperatures and changing foliage. Avoid winter due to cold weather and potential snow.

Tips

- **Wear appropriate clothing:** Layers are essential, as the temperature can vary significantly between the woods and the beach. Sturdy shoes with good traction are recommended.
- **Consider the time of day:** Early morning or late afternoon hikes can be more pleasant, especially during hot summer months.
- **Stay on the trail:** Protect the delicate ecosystem by staying on designated paths.
- **Be aware of wildlife:** You might encounter various wildlife, including birds, deer, and even the occasional coyote. Observe from a distance and do not disturb them.
- **Respect other hikers:** Be mindful of your noise level and yield the trail to those going uphill.
- **Take your time:** Enjoy the scenery and take breaks to appreciate the natural beauty.
- **Explore both loops:** The short loop around the wetlands is a great option for families or those with limited time. The longer loop to the beach offers a more challenging hike with stunning rewards.
- **Wildlife watching:** Keep an eye out for birds, especially in the wetland areas. You might also spot deer, turtles, and other creatures.
- **Photography:** The trail offers plenty of photo opportunities, from lush greenery to breathtaking lake views.

- **Beach time:** If you choose to hike to the beach, make sure to pack your swimsuit and towel for a refreshing dip.

Pinhook Bog Trails

Location

Pinhook Bog is located within Indiana Dunes National Park, near La Porte, Indiana.

Trailhead

The trailhead for the Upland Trail is at the Pinhook Bog parking lot.

Description

The Pinhook Bog Trail System offers two distinct experiences:

- **Upland Trail:** This 2.1-mile trail winds through a beech and maple forest, providing a glimpse into the glacial moraine's history.

- **Bog Trail:** A unique 0.9-mile boardwalk journey through a fascinating bog ecosystem, featuring carnivorous plants and other rare species.

Difficulty

- **Upland Trail:** Easy to moderate with some elevation changes.

- **Bog Trail:** Easy on the boardwalk, but requires ranger-led access.

Type of Hike

- **Upland Trail:** Out and back.

- **Bog Trail:** Out and back (ranger-led).

Elevation Change

Moderate elevation changes on the Upland Trail. The Bog Trail is relatively flat.

- **Upland Trail: No dogs allowed.**

- **Bog Trail: No dogs allowed.**

- **Upland Trail: Suitable for kids with appropriate supervision.**

- **Bog Trail: Suitable for older, curious kids on ranger-led tours.**

Length

- **Upland Trail:** 2.1 miles.

- **Bog Trail:** 0.9 miles.

Estimated Time to Complete

- **Upland Trail:** Approximately 1.5 hours.

- **Bog Trail:** Approximately 1 hour (ranger-led).

Accessibility

- **Upland Trail:** Accessible to most people.

- **Bog Trail:** Not accessible without a ranger-led tour.

Equipment Needed

- **Upland Trail:** Comfortable hiking shoes, water, insect repellent.

- **Bog Trail:** No personal equipment needed, as it's a ranger-led tour.

Ability

- **Upland Trail:** Suitable for most fitness levels.

- **Bog Trail:** Requires participation in a ranger-led program.

Features

- **Upland Trail:** Scenic forest, wildlife viewing opportunities.

- **Bog Trail:** Unique ecosystem, carnivorous plants, educational experience.

Allowed Uses

- **Upland Trail:** Hiking.

- **Bog Trail:** Hiking (ranger-led only).

Trail Surface

- **Upland Trail:** Packed dirt.

- **Bog Trail:** Boardwalk.

Best Time to Hike

- **Upland Trail:** Spring and fall for pleasant weather.

- **Bog Trail:** Summer weekends during ranger-led programs.

Important Note: The Bog Trail is only accessible during ranger-led programs due to its delicate ecosystem.

Essential Gear:

- **Waterproof boots:** Essential for the Bog Trail, as the boardwalk can be submerged.

- **Insect repellent:** Mosquitoes and ticks are prevalent, especially in warmer months.

- **Long pants and sleeves:** Protect against ticks and poison ivy.

- **Camera:** Capture the stunning beauty of the bog.

Upland Trail: Can be wet and muddy, especially after rain.

Bog Trail: A floating boardwalk that submerges when walked on.

Stay on the trail: Protect the fragile habitat by staying on designated paths.

Learn about the bog: Research the unique ecosystem and its inhabitants before your hike.

Combine with other hikes: Explore other trails in the Indiana Dunes National Park to make a full day of it.

Portage Lakefront and Riverwalk Trail

Location

Portage, Indiana, within the Indiana Dunes National Park.

Trailhead

The trailhead is located within the Portage Lakefront and Riverwalk Park. There is ample paved parking available.

Description

A scenic trail that offers a mix of lakefront views, restored dune habitat, and boardwalk sections. It's a popular spot for leisurely walks, birdwatching, and enjoying the beauty of Lake Michigan.

Difficulty

Easy. There are minimal elevation changes and the trail is well-maintained.

Type of Hike

Loop. The trail forms a loop, allowing you to return to the starting point.

Elevation Change

Minimal. The trail is relatively flat.

Dogs are allowed on leash.

The easy terrain and scenic views make it a great option for families.

Length

0.9 miles

Estimated Time to Complete

Approximately 45 minutes.

Accessibility

The trail is mostly wheelchair accessible, with some sections of boardwalk and one set of stairs.

Equipment Needed

Comfortable walking shoes, water, sunscreen, and sunglasses.

Ability

Suitable for all ages and fitness levels.

Features

- Scenic views of Lake Michigan
- Restored dune habitat
- Boardwalk sections
- Accessible fishing pier
- Public pavilion with restrooms and seasonal snack bar

Allowed Uses

Hiking, walking, birdwatching, fishing. Bicycles and motorized vehicles are prohibited.

Trail Surface

Paved with some sections of boardwalk.

Best Time to Hike

The trail is enjoyable year-round. Spring and fall offer beautiful colors, while summer provides opportunities for swimming and sunbathing. Winter can be picturesque with the possibility of seeing ice formations on the lake.

- **Parking:** There are three paved parking lots available. Arrive early on weekends and holidays to secure a spot.
- **Beach Time:** Relax on the sandy shores, swim, or build sandcastles.
- **Birdwatching:** The area is known for its diverse bird population. Bring binoculars to spot different species.
- **Fishing:** The accessible fishing pier provides a great opportunity to cast a line.
- **Picnicking:** Find a spot on the beach or in the pavilion to enjoy a meal with a view.
- **Wear Comfortable Shoes:** The trail surface is paved, but there are some sections of boardwalk and stairs.
- **Bring Sunscreen and Insect Repellent:** Protect yourself from the sun and bugs, especially during warmer months.
- Restrooms and potable water are available at the pavilion.
- The pavilion also has a seasonal snack bar.

Tolleston Dunes Trail

Location

Indiana Dunes National Park, near Ogden Dunes, Indiana.

Trailhead

Located off US-12, also known as Dunes Highway.

Description

The Tolleston Dunes Trail winds through 4,700-year-old sand dunes, offering stunning views of diverse habitats including black oak savanna, wetlands, and unique plant life like prickly pear cactus and wild blue lupine. The trail provides a glimpse into the changing shoreline of Lake Michigan.

Difficulty

Moderate. The trail involves consistent changes in elevation due to the dune landscape.

Type of Hike

Loop or out and back.

Elevation Change

Moderate elevation changes due to the nature of the dunes.

Dogs must be on a leash (6 feet or shorter).

It is kid friendly but younger children might find the sand and some inclines challenging.

Length

Approximately 2.9 miles.

Estimated Time to Complete

Around 2 hours.

Accessibility

The trail itself is not accessible, but there is a wheelchair-accessible picnic area and overlook near the trailhead.

Equipment Needed

Sturdy hiking shoes, water, sunscreen, insect repellent, and a hat.

Ability

Moderate fitness level is recommended due to the changing elevation.

Features

Scenic views, diverse wildlife, unique plant life.

Allowed Uses

Hiking. Bicycles and motorized vehicles are prohibited.

Trail Surface

Sand with some sections of packed soil, gravel, and boardwalk. Boardwalk can be submerged.

Best Time to Hike

Spring and fall offer pleasant temperatures and vibrant colors. Summer can be hot and sandy, while winter may be cold and windy.

Tips

- **Check the weather:** Dunes can be exposed and windy, especially near the lake. Dress accordingly.
- **Wear appropriate footwear:** Hiking boots or sturdy shoes with good ankle support are recommended due to the varying terrain.
- **Bring water and snacks:** There are no facilities on the trail, so come prepared.
- **Protect yourself:** Sunscreen, insect repellent, and a hat are essential, especially during warmer months.
- **Consider the time of day:** Early morning or late afternoon can be less crowded and offer better lighting for photography.
- **Watch your step:** The trail is uneven with sand, rocks, and roots. Be cautious to avoid falls.
- **Stay on the trail:** Protect delicate dune ecosystems by staying on designated paths.
- **Take your time:** Enjoy the scenery and take breaks to appreciate the natural beauty.
- **Choose your route:** Decide if you want to hike the entire 2.9-mile loop or take the shorter 2.1-mile option.
- **Bring binoculars:** Birdwatching is a popular activity in the area.
- **Capture the moment:** Take photos to remember your adventure.
- **Check for trail closures:** Occasionally, trails may be closed due to weather or other conditions.

West Beach Trails

Location

West Beach is located in the Indiana Dunes National Park, near Portage, Indiana.

Trailhead

The trailhead for West Beach Trails is located at the West Beach parking area within the Indiana Dunes National Park.

Description

West Beach offers a diverse hiking experience, combining beach relaxation with exploration of various habitats. It features three interconnected loops: Dune Succession, West Beach, and Long Lake. Each loop provides unique views, from towering dunes to serene lakeside settings.

Difficulty

- **Dune Succession Trail:** Moderate. Includes a steep climb with 270+ stairs.

- **West Beach Trail:** Easy. Primarily flat with loose sand.

- **Long Lake Trail:** Moderate. Some elevation changes and varying terrain.

Overall, the trails can be enjoyed by a range of fitness levels, as there are options for different abilities.

Type of Hike

Loop trails.

Elevation Change

Significant elevation change on the Dune Succession Trail due to the dune climb. The other two loops have more gradual elevation changes.

Dogs are allowed on leash (6 feet or shorter).

The West Beach Trail is generally kid-friendly. The Dune Succession Trail might be challenging for younger children due to the stairs.

Length

- **3-loop:** 3.4 miles

- **Dune Succession:** 0.9 miles

- **West Beach:** 1.2 miles

- **Long Lake:** 2.2 miles

Estimated Time to Complete

45 minutes to 2.5 hours depending on the chosen loop(s) and pace.

Accessibility

The West Beach Trail is relatively accessible. The Dune Succession Trail has stairs and might be challenging for individuals with mobility issues.

Equipment Needed

- Sturdy hiking shoes

- Water

- Sunscreen

- Insect repellent

- Hat

Ability

Varying abilities can enjoy the West Beach Trails. The Dune Succession Trail is more challenging, while the other two loops are suitable for most hikers.

Features

- Scenic views of Lake Michigan, dunes, forests, and Long Lake

- Diverse habitats (dunes, pine forest, oak savanna, wetland)

- Beach access

- Potential for wildlife sightings

Allowed Uses

Hiking is the primary activity. Bicycles are not allowed on the trails.

Trail Surface

Packed dirt with some sections of loose sand.

Best Time to Hike

Spring and fall offer pleasant temperatures and vibrant foliage. Summer is ideal for beach activities. Winter can be challenging due to weather conditions, but offers unique landscapes.

- **Choose Your Loop:** Consider your fitness level and time available when selecting the Dune Succession, West Beach, or Long Lake Loop.
- **Check Weather Conditions:** Lake Michigan weather can change rapidly. Dress in layers and be prepared for wind and potential rain.
- **Watch Your Step:** The trails can be sandy and uneven, especially on the dunes. Wear appropriate footwear.
- **Take Breaks:** Enjoy the stunning views and take breaks to rest and recharge.
- **Beach Time:** After your hike, relax on the beach and enjoy the refreshing water.
- **Picnic:** Bring a picnic lunch and enjoy a meal with a view.
- **Pets:** Leashed dogs are allowed on the trails, but they are prohibited in the swimming area during the summer.

The Dunes Succession Trail

Biking Trails

Calumet Bike Trail

Location

The Calumet Bike Trail runs through Indiana Dunes National Park, along the southern border of the park. It stretches from Dune Acres in the west to the Town of Pines in the east.

Trailhead

- **West Trailhead:** 1184 North Mineral Springs Road, Dune Acres, IN 46304

- **East Trailhead:** 2752 U.S. Highway 12, Town of Pines, IN 46360

Description

The Calumet Bike Trail is a 19-mile gravel trail that follows the South Shore Railroad tracks and NIPSCO power lines. It offers a flat, easy ride through a diverse landscape of wetlands, prairies, and dunes. While it doesn't provide the dramatic views of the lake, it offers a quieter, more secluded experience.

Difficulty

Easy

Type of Hike

Out and back

Elevation Change

Minimal elevation change

Dogs are allowed on leash.

The trail is generally flat and easy, making it suitable for kids.

71

Length

19 miles

Estimated Time to Complete

1.5 to 2 hours

Accessibility

The trail is primarily gravel and may have standing water in some areas, making it less accessible for those with mobility issues.

Equipment Needed

Mountain bike or hybrid bike, helmet, water, sunscreen, insect repellent

Ability

Beginner to intermediate cyclists

Features

- Wetlands
- Prairies
- Diverse wildlife

Allowed Uses

Hiking and cycling

Trail Surface

Gravel

Best Time to Cycle

Spring, summer, and fall are ideal times to cycle on the Calumet Bike Trail. Avoid riding during wet conditions as the trail can become muddy and impassable.

Tips

Bike Choice and Preparation

- **Gravel bike or mountain bike:** Road bikes are not recommended due to the trail's condition.

- **Wide tires:** These will help you navigate the uneven gravel and potential standing water.

- **Fenders:** Highly recommended to protect yourself from spray.

- **Bike maintenance:** Ensure your bike is in good condition, especially brakes and tires.

Trail Conditions and Safety

- **Be aware of trail conditions:** The trail can be muddy and have standing water, especially after rain.

- **Ride with caution:** The gravel surface can be uneven and rough, so watch your speed.

- **Wear a helmet:** Always protect your head.

- **Visibility:** Wear bright clothing, especially if riding in low light conditions.

- **Wildlife:** Be mindful of wildlife and give them plenty of space.

Enjoy the Ride

- **Take your time:** The Calumet Bike Trail is a scenic route, so enjoy the views.

- **Bring water and snacks:** Stay hydrated and fueled.

- **Consider bikepacking:** The trail's length and remote nature make it a great option for bikepacking.

Dunes Kankakee Bike Trail

Trailhead

- **North:** Indiana Dunes State Park fee collection parking lot

- **South:** Indiana Dunes Visitor Center

Description

The Dunes Kankakee Bike Trail is a paved path that runs along State Road 49, connecting the Indiana Dunes State Park to the Indiana Dunes Visitor Center. It offers a scenic ride through the diverse landscapes of the park, including wetlands, forests, and open dunes.

Difficulty

Easy with a few short inclines when crossing bridges over US Highway 12 and 20.

Type of Hike

Out and back

Elevation Change

Minimal, except for the two bridge crossings.

Dogs are allowed on leash (6 feet or shorter).

The trail is easy and suitable for children of all ages.

Length

3.6 miles

Estimated Time to Complete

Approximately 30 minutes

Accessibility

The trail is paved and accessible to most people.

Equipment Needed

Bicycle, helmet, water, sunscreen, insect repellent

Ability

Beginner to intermediate cyclists

Features

- Scenic views of the park
- Connection to the Calumet Bike Trail and South Shore Railroad train station

Allowed Uses

Biking, walking, running

Trail Surface

Paved

Best Time to Cycle

Spring, summer, and fall offer pleasant weather for cycling. Avoid winter months due to potential icy conditions.

Tips

- **Consider bike rental:** If you don't have your own bike, there are bike rental options available in the area.
- **Enjoy the scenery:** Take your time and appreciate the natural beauty around you.
- **Watch for wildlife:** Keep an eye out for birds, deer, and other wildlife that call the park home.
- **Be mindful of other trail users:** Share the trail with pedestrians and other cyclists.
- **Stay hydrated:** Drink plenty of water, especially on hot days.
- **Take breaks:** There are plenty of places to stop and rest along the trail.
- **Connect with other trails:** The Dunes Kankakee Trail connects to the Calumet Bike Trail, offering more opportunities for exploration.
- **Combine with other activities:** Consider combining your bike ride with a visit to the beach, hiking, or birdwatching.

Porter Brickyard Bike Trail

Location and Trailhead

The Porter Brickyard Bike Trail is located in Porter County, Indiana, and runs through the town of Porter.

- **North Trailhead:** 1184 North Mineral Springs Road, Dune Acres, IN 46304

- **South Trailhead:** 198 South Jackson Boulevard, Chesterton, IN 46304

Description

The Porter Brickyard Bike Trail is a paved, 7-mile trail connecting the Calumet Trail in the north and the Prairie Duneland Trail in the south. It offers a scenic ride through urban and suburban areas, with views of the Little Calumet River and Mnoké Prairie. The trail also connects to other trails within the Indiana Dunes National Park.

Difficulty

Easy to moderate. While the trail is mostly flat, there are some gentle inclines and declines.

Type of Hike

Out and back or one-way, depending on your starting point.

Elevation Change

Minimal elevation change, making it suitable for riders of all levels.

Dogs are allowed on the trail, but they must be leashed.

The trail is generally safe and easy for children.

Length

7 miles

Estimated Time to Complete

Approximately 30 minutes to complete the entire trail.

Accessibility

The trail is fully paved and accessible to people with disabilities.

Equipment Needed

Bicycle, helmet, water, and sunscreen.

Ability

Suitable for riders of all levels.

Features

- Scenic views of the Little Calumet River and Mnoké Prairie

- Connects to other trails in the Indiana Dunes National Park

- Urban and suburban setting

Allowed Uses

Cycling and walking/hiking.

Trail Surface

Paved

Best Time to Cycle

The trail is enjoyable year-round, but spring and fall offer pleasant weather conditions.

Tips

- **Enjoy the scenery:** Take your time to appreciate the natural beauty around you.
- **Be aware of your surroundings:** Watch out for pedestrians, other cyclists, and wildlife.
- **Observe trail etiquette:** Yield to hikers and other trail users.
- **Stay on the designated trail:** Avoid riding on fragile ecosystems.
- **Take breaks:** Stop and rest when needed, especially on hot days.

- **Explore connections:** The Porter Brickyard Trail connects to other trails, so consider extending your ride.
- **Best time to ride:** Early morning or late afternoon can be ideal to avoid crowds and enjoy cooler temperatures.
- **Wildlife:** You might encounter various wildlife, such as deer, birds, and turtles. Observe them from a distance and avoid disturbing their habitat.
- **Photography:** Bring a camera to capture the stunning scenery.
- **Combine with other activities:** After your ride, consider visiting the beach, hiking, or exploring the nearby towns.

Prairie Duneland Bike Trail

Trailhead

It offers two trailheads:

- **East Trailhead:** 198 South Jackson Boulevard, Chesterton, IN 46304

- **West Trailhead:** 4 North Hobart Road, Hobart, IN 46342

Description

The Prairie Duneland Bike Trail is a paved, flat rail trail that offers a scenic ride through diverse landscapes including prairies, forests, and residential areas. It's a popular choice for cyclists, runners, and walkers.

Difficulty

Easy

Type of Hike

Out and back or **loop** (depending on your starting point and desired route)

Elevation Change

Minimal (approximately 30 feet of elevation gain)

Dogs are allowed on leash.

The trail is flat and easy, making it suitable for kids of all ages.

Length

22.4 miles (round trip)

Estimated Time to Complete

2 hours (average biking time)

Accessibility

The trail is wheelchair accessible.

Equipment Needed

- Bike (recommended)
- Helmet
- Water
- Sunscreen
- Insect repellent

Ability

The trail is suitable for riders of all abilities.

Features

- Scenic views of prairies, forests, and residential areas
- Family-friendly
- Multiple parking areas with picnic shelters, restrooms, and drinking fountains

Allowed Uses

- Biking

- Hiking

- Running

- Walking

Trail Surface

Paved

Best Time to Cycle

The trail is enjoyable year-round, but spring and fall offer pleasant temperatures and beautiful scenery.

Tips

- The trail is relatively flat and easy, making it suitable for riders of all levels. Consider your fitness level and time available when planning your route.
- **Trailhead Options:** The trail has multiple access points. Choose a starting point based on your location and desired ride length.
- **Bike Rental:** If you don't have your own bike, there are bike rental options available in the area.
- **Weather Check:** Check the weather forecast before heading out. Rain can make the trail slippery.
- **Safety First:** Wear a helmet and follow traffic rules. Be aware of other trail users, including pedestrians, runners, and cyclists.
- **Hydration and Snacks:** Bring plenty of water and snacks, especially if you're planning a longer ride.
- **Sun Protection:** Don't forget sunscreen, sunglasses, and a hat, especially on sunny days.

- **Explore Side Trails:** Take advantage of the opportunity to explore side trails and discover hidden gems.
- **Trail Etiquette:** Be courteous to other trail users. Yield to pedestrians and slower cyclists.

Marquette Bike Trail

Location

The Marquette Bike Trail is located within the Indiana Dunes National Park, specifically in the Gary area.

Trailhead

There are two trailheads:

- **East Trailhead:** 540 North County Line Road, Gary, IN 46403

- **West Trailhead:** No parking available.

Description

The Marquette Bike Trail is a former railroad right-of-way that has been converted into a trail. It offers a glimpse into the industrial history of the region while providing access to the natural beauty of the dunes.

Difficulty

Moderate. While the trail is mostly flat, some sections may have loose gravel or uneven terrain.

Type of Hike

Out and back.

Elevation Change

Minimal elevation change.

Dogs are allowed on leash.

Kids can enjoy the trail, but adult supervision is recommended.

Length

4.6 miles.

Estimated Time to Complete

Approximately 30 minutes.

Accessibility

The trail is not accessible to wheelchairs.

Equipment Needed

Bike, helmet, water, sunscreen, insect repellent.

Ability

Intermediate biking skills are recommended.

Features

- Industrial history
- Proximity to Lake Michigan
- Opportunity for birdwatching

Allowed Uses

Hiking, biking.

Trail Surface

Gravel.

Best Time to Cycle

Spring, summer, and fall are ideal times to cycle on the Marquette Bike Trail. Avoid winter due to potential weather conditions.

Tips

- **Tire Pressure:** Given the trail's varied terrain, consider running slightly lower tire pressure for better traction.

- **Gear Selection:** A wide gear range is beneficial to tackle both flat sections and potential sandy areas.

- **Bike Condition:** Ensure your bike is in good working order, especially brakes and drivetrain.

- **Respect Nature:** Indiana Dunes is a delicate ecosystem. Stay on the designated trails to protect the environment.
- **Watch for Wildlife:** You might encounter various wildlife, including deer, birds, and small mammals. Be cautious and respectful of their habitat.
- **Be Prepared for Varying Terrain:** The trail includes flat sections, sandy stretches, and some elevation changes. Adjust your riding style accordingly.
- **Hydration and Sun Protection:** Bring plenty of water, especially on hot days. Don't forget sunscreen and a hat.
- **Bike Etiquette:** Share the trail with other users, including hikers and pedestrians. Be courteous and announce your presence when approaching others.
- **Parking:** While there is parking available at the east trailhead, options may be limited at the west end.
- **Facilities:** There are no restrooms or water fountains along the trail, so come prepared.

Oak Savannah Bike Trail

Location and Trailhead

The Oak Savannah Bike Trail is located within the Hobart Prairie Grove unit of Indiana Dunes National Park. It offers two trailheads:

- **East Trailhead:** 4 North Hobart Road, Hobart, IN 46342

- **West Trailhead:** 301 South Colfax Street, Griffith, IN 46319

Description

The Oak Savannah Bike Trail is a paved, flat, and relatively easy trail that meanders through a diverse landscape of oak savanna, prairies, and wetlands. It's a popular choice for cyclists, runners, and walkers alike.

Difficulty

Easy

Type of Hike

Out and back

Elevation Change

Minimal. The trail is very flat.

Dogs are welcomed but must be leashed.

This trail is perfect for families with children.

Length

17.8 miles (round trip)

Estimated Time to Complete

Approximately 2 hours (bike ride)

Accessibility

The trail is fully paved and accessible to most individuals.

Equipment Needed

Bike (for cycling), helmet, water, sunscreen, and insect repellent.

Ability

Beginner to intermediate cyclists. Walkers and runners of all levels can enjoy the trail.

Features

- Scenic views of prairies and wetlands
- Opportunity to see wildlife
- Connection to other trails

Allowed Uses

Hiking, biking, running, walking

Trail Surface

Paved

Best Time to Cycle

Spring, summer, and fall offer pleasant riding conditions. Avoid winter months due to potential icy conditions.

Note: While the Oak Savannah Bike Trail is primarily within the park, it does connect to other trails outside the park boundaries.

- **Check Trail Conditions:** While the Oak Savannah Bike Trail is generally well-maintained, weather conditions can affect the trail. Check the National Park Service website or local news for any trail closures or advisories.
- **Gear Up:** Ensure your bike is in good working condition, including tires, brakes, and gears. Wear a helmet, comfortable clothing, and consider gloves for added protection.
- **Hydrate and Nourish:** Bring plenty of water, especially on warmer days. Pack energy snacks for longer rides.
- **Know the Rules:** Familiarize yourself with park regulations, including permitted bike types, leash laws for pets, and any specific rules for the Oak Savannah Bike Trail.
- **Be Mindful of Others:** Share the trail with other users, including hikers, runners, and horseback riders. Yield to slower traffic and use a bell to alert others of your presence.
- **Take Your Time:** Enjoy the scenery! The Oak Savannah Bike Trail offers beautiful views, so take your time to appreciate the surroundings.
- **Be Prepared for Weather:** The weather can change quickly, so be prepared for rain or sun. Pack accordingly.
- **Safety First:** Ride defensively and be aware of your surroundings. Watch for potential hazards, such as roots, rocks, or uneven surfaces.
- **Combine with Other Trails:** The Oak Savannah Bike Trail connects to other trails in the area, allowing you to extend your ride.

Camping

Dunewood Campground

Basic Information

- **Number of sites:** 66 (53 drive-in, 13 walk-in)

- **Electric hookups:** None

- **RVs:** Allowed, but some sites have length restrictions

- **Tents:** Allowed

- **Walk-in:** 13 sites

- **Group sites:** None

- **Horse camping:** Not allowed

Campground Features

- **Amenities:** Restrooms, hot showers

- **Toilet type:** Flush toilets

- **Shower type:** Hot showers

- **Water facilities:** Potable water available

Operation Seasons

- Open: April to October

- Closed: November to March

Fees

- Fees vary depending on the season and type of site. Check the official Indiana Dunes National Park website for the most up-to-date pricing.

Accessibility

- **Wheelchair access:** Four sites are wheelchair accessible (numbers 15, 30, 41, and 55)

- **RV and trailer:** Allowed, but some sites have length restrictions

- **Campground classification:** Developed (restrooms, showers)

Reservations

- Reservations are required and can be made through Recreation.gov.

Note: While Dunewood Campground offers a more natural camping experience without electric hookups, it's still considered a developed campground due to the presence of restrooms and showers.

Indiana Dunes State Park Campground

Basic Information

- **Number of Sites:** 247

- **Electric Hookups:** All sites

- **RVs:** Allowed

- **Tents:** Allowed

- **Walk-in:** Not applicable

- **Group:** Not available

- **Horse:** Not allowed

Campground Features

- **Amenities:** Modern restrooms, shower houses, electric hookups, picnic tables, fire rings

- **Toilet Type:** Modern flush toilets

- **Shower Type:** Hot showers

- **Water Facilities:** Potable water available

Operation Seasons

- Open year-round

Fees

- Fees vary depending on the season and whether you are an Indiana resident or non-resident. Check the official website for the most up-to-date pricing information.

Accessibility

- **Wheelchair Access:** The campground is wheelchair accessible, with accessible restrooms and showers.

- **RV and Trailer:** The campground can accommodate RVs and trailers.

- **Campground Classification:** Developed

Reservations

- Reservations are highly recommended, especially during peak seasons. You can make reservations through the Indiana State Parks reservation system.

Note: While there have been some reports of bathroom and shower issues in the past, it's important to note that these are isolated incidents. The campground generally maintains clean and well-maintained facilities.

Dunbar Group Site

Basic Information

- **Number of sites:** 1 (group site)

- **Electric hookups:** None

- **RVs:** Not allowed

- **Tents:** Allowed

- **Walk-in:** Yes

- **Group:** Yes (up to 30 people)

- **Horse:** Not allowed

Campground Features

- **Amenities:** Picnic tables, fire ring

- **Toilet type:** Restrooms located in Dunbar Beach parking lot (400 feet away)

- **Shower type:** No showers available

- **Water facilities:** Water available at Dunbar Beach parking lot (400 feet away)

Operation Seasons

- Year-round

Fees

- Check the official Indiana Dunes National Park website or Recreation.gov for current fee information.

Accessibility Information

- **Wheelchair access:** Not specifically mentioned, but given the nature of a beachside group site, access might be limited.

- **RV and trailer:** Not allowed.

- **Campground classification:** Primitive

Reservations

- Reservations are required and can be made through Recreation.gov

Central Avenue Walk-in Sites

Basic Information

- **Number of Sites:** 5

- **Electric Hookups:** None

- **RVs:** Not allowed

- **Tents:** Allowed

- **Walk-in:** Required

- **Group:** No

- **Horse:** Not allowed

Campground Features

- **Amenities:** Picnic table, fire pit

- **Toilet Type:** Vault toilet

- **Shower Type:** None

- **Water Facilities:** None (bring your own water)

Operation Seasons

- Typically, open seasonally, but exact dates can vary. It's best to check the official Indiana Dunes National Park website for the most current information.

Fees

- Fees can change annually. It's recommended to check the official Indiana Dunes National Park website or Recreation.gov for the most up-to-date fee information.

Accessibility Information

- **Wheelchair Access:** Not accessible. The terrain involves walking over dunes and uneven ground.

- **RV and Trailer:** Not allowed.

- **Campground Classification:** Primitive

Reservations

- Reservations are recommended and can be made through Recreation.gov.

Glossary

Campground classification - Campgrounds have been classified into two main types: developed and primitive

Developed Campgrounds

Developed campgrounds are those that offer a variety of amenities and facilities to campers. These amenities can vary depending on the specific campground, but they typically include:

- Designated campsites: These are marked areas where campers can pitch their tents, park their RVs, or set up other camping shelters.

- Restrooms: Developed campgrounds will have restrooms with flush toilets and running water. Some campgrounds may also have vault toilets, which are self-contained toilets that do not require plumbing.

- Water: Developed campgrounds will have a source of clean drinking water, such as a well or spigot.

- Picnic tables and fire rings: Most developed campgrounds will have picnic tables and fire rings at each campsite.

- Other amenities: Some developed campgrounds may also offer other amenities, such as showers, laundry facilities, camp stores, playgrounds, and swimming pools.

Primitive Campgrounds

Primitive campgrounds, on the other hand, offer few or no amenities. These campgrounds are typically located in more remote areas and are designed for campers who are looking for a more rustic camping experience. Primitive campgrounds may have some or all of the following:

- Designated campsites: Some primitive campgrounds may have designated campsites, but these are often simply cleared areas of land.
- Fire rings: Primitive campgrounds may have fire rings, but this is not always the case.
- No amenities: Primitive campgrounds typically do not have any other amenities, such as restrooms, water, picnic tables, or trash collection.

Trail difficulty - refers to a rating system that helps hikers choose trails that are appropriate for their fitness level and experience. Here's a breakdown of common trail difficulty categories:

Easy: Easy trails are generally short (less than 2 miles) and have a flat or gentle incline. They are suitable for hikers of all ages and fitness levels, including young children and families.

Moderate: Moderate trails are moderately challenging and may be longer (2 to 4 miles) with some steeper sections and elevation gain. They are suitable for hikers in good physical condition who are comfortable walking for a few hours.

Challenging: Challenging trails are more difficult and may be longer (4+ miles) with significant elevation gain, steep inclines, and uneven terrain. They require good physical fitness and some experience hiking on challenging terrain.

Strenuous: Strenuous trails are the most difficult and are typically long (4+ miles) with significant elevation gain, steep inclines, and difficult terrain. They require excellent physical fitness, strong hiking skills, and experience navigating difficult trails.

Elevation change - This is the overall variation in height you'll experience on the trail. It considers both going up (elevation gain) and going down (elevation loss).

Features- is simply any interesting or noteworthy aspect of the trail itself. This could include things like scenic overlooks, waterfalls, wildflowers, or historical markers.

Loop Hike - is a more intricate and diverse form of hiking. As the name suggests, in a Loop hike, you start and finish at the same trailhead, but you follow a circuitous route that doesn't require retracing your steps. Here are the characteristics that make Loop hikes appealing:

1. **Variety**: Loop hikes offer a rich diversity of scenery, as you traverse different terrains, ecosystems, and vistas. You won't see the same section of the trail twice.

2. **Sense of Accomplishment**: Completing a loop hike often feels more satisfying, as you've circumnavigated a specific area and returned to your starting point without repeating any segments of the trail.

3. **Adventure**: The element of uncertainty and exploration is more prominent in loop hikes, as you might not know exactly what's around each bend. This adds excitement and a spirit of adventure to the experience.

4. **Efficiency**: Loop hikes make efficient use of your time and energy since they don't require doubling back. This can be especially appealing when you have a limited amount of time for your hike.

However, Loop hikes also have their challenges, such as potentially more complex navigation and the need for good trail markers. Some hikers might find the unpredictability of the terrain and the possibility of getting lost a bit daunting.

Out and Back Hike

The "Out and Back" hike, also known as a "there and back" hike, is one of the simplest and most straightforward hiking formats. In this type of hike, you begin at a designated trailhead and travel along the path until you decide to turn around and return to your starting point. Here are some key features of Out and Back hikes:

1. **Simplicity**: Out and Back hikes are ideal for beginners and those who prefer a straightforward, no-fuss approach. Since you retrace your steps, navigation is often more straightforward, reducing the chances of getting lost.

2. **Predictable Terrain**: Knowing that you'll return on the same trail means you have a good understanding of the terrain. This allows you to plan and pace your hike more accurately.

3. **Scenic Views**: Out and Back hikes often lead you to the same stunning viewpoints on your return journey, offering a different perspective of the landscape you've just traversed.

4. **Flexibility**: You can customize the length of your hike by choosing how far you want to venture from the trailhead, making it suitable for hikers of all levels.

However, there are limitations to Out and Back hikes. The monotony of retracing your steps can become less engaging for some, and the predictability of the terrain might not provide the variety that loop hikes offer.

Point to Point Hike

Refers to a hike that starts at one location and ends at a different location. This means you won't be following the same path back to your starting point like you would with a loop trail. Because of this, point-to-point hikes often require some logistical planning to get back to your car or starting point.

Key features:

1. **Transportation:** You'll need a way to get back to where you parked your car at the beginning of the hike. This could involve arranging a shuttle service with a friend, using public transportation if available, or having another car pick you up at the end point.

2. **Multi-day hikes:** Point-to-point trails are commonly used for multi-day backpacking trips, where you camp overnight along the way.

Overlook - refers to a specific location on a trail that offers a particularly scenic or panoramic view of the surrounding landscape. These are often high points, such as cliffs or mountain summits, that provide unobstructed vistas.

Hikers often aim for overlooks as a reward for their effort on the trail. They can be a great place to take a break, enjoy the scenery, and snap some pictures.

RV Sites - RV sites are designated areas within a campground or RV park specifically designed to accommodate recreational vehicles (RVs) like motorhomes, travel trailers, and fifth-wheel trailers.

Tent Sites - A tent site is a designated area within a campground specifically designed for pitching tents. These sites typically have a cleared, level area of ground suitable for setting up a tent, and may also include amenities like a fire ring, picnic table, and sometimes a lantern post.

Trailhead – refers to the starting point of a trail. It's essentially the place where you leave the road or developed area and begin your trek on the designated path.

Made in the USA
Monee, IL
21 May 2025

17872455R10059